LIBERTY

Mary Martina Dockter

ISBN 979-8-99072-979-7 (paperback)
ISBN 979-8-99072-976-6 (eBook)

Copyright © 2024 by Mary Martina Dockter

All rights reserved. No part of this publication may be reproduced, distributed, or transmitted in any form or by any means, including photocopying, recording, or other electronic or mechanical methods without the prior written permission of the publisher.

DEDICATED TO THE MEN AND
WOMEN WHO HAVE SERVED
AND FOUGHT FOR OUR FREEDOM

Contents

LIBERTY	1
UNITED STATES	2
WE THE PEOPLE	3
LONG LIVE LIBERTY	4
STARS AND STRIPES	5
FOREVER FREE	6
LEARN TO FLY	7
EAGLE FREE	8
EAGLE EYE	9
OUR BIRTHRIGHT	10
THE FREE	11
LIBERTY FREE	12
LET FREEDOM RING	13
PATRIOTISM	14
FREEDOM	15
DIAMOND IN THE ROUGH	16
PATRIOT	17
A CITIZEN TO BE AND THE THREE COUNTRIES	18
SURVIVOR	19
CONSTRUCTION OF AMERICA	20
OUR REPUBLIC	21
LIBERTY LIGHTS	22
LAND OF GIANTS	23
CONSTITUTIONAL	24
LESSONS OF THE FREE	25
DECLARATION	27
AMUCK	28
VOICE OF FREEDOM	29
DON'T TREAD ON ME	30
FOREFATHERS' FRAME	31
FRAMEWORK	32
200 YEAR WARRANTY	33

DEATH OF A NATION	34
AMERICA'S OBITUARY	35
BLINDSIDED	36
PINOCCHIOBAMA	37
ROOTED	39
DEFIANCE	40
A CIVIL CRY	41
AUTARKY	43
TWIST OF FATE	44
GHOSTLY GROUNDS	46
SACRED SOIL	47
PAID IN FULL	48
DEBT FREE	49
HUMBLE PIE	50
WALK THROUGH TIME	51
LIVE AND LEARN	52
HISTORY'S LESSON	53
EVOLUTION OF WAR	54
WHY	55
HUMAN WALL	56
SILENCE SPEAKS	57
FREEDOM'S DECREE	58
CALL OF THE FREE	59
WILDERNESS WITHIN	60
FEARLESS	61
CRY OF THE FREE	62
LIBERTY'S SPOKEN	63
LIBERTY BROKEN	64
UNITED WE STAND	65
DIVIDED WE FALL	66
LIVE AND LET BE	67
DREAM ON	68
MY CHOICE	69
LET ME BE	70
ONE ARE WE	71
OWNERSHIP	72

WE ARE ONE	73
TO BE HONEST	74
HONESTY	75
CRIES OF LIES	76
BURRO BUREAUCRACY	77
ZOMBIES vs. VAMPIRES	78
PACHYDERM POLITICS	79
RIGHTEOUSNESS	80
STATUE OF FREEDOM	81
MILITARY MIGHT	82
COURAGE	83
MY DAD	84
KNEW HE MUST GO	85
SLOGORN	86
THE DIE CRY	87
BEAUTY BLOOMED	88
POPPY	89
OPERATION DETACHMENT	90
RED, WHITE AND BLUE	91
MEDAL OF HONOR	92
BEYOND BRAVERY	93
ABOUT FACE	94
PRISONER OF WAR	95
LEFT TO ONESELF	97
UP IN ARMS	98
CRY OF INNOCENCE	101
DEVIL DEVIL	102
WARFARE'S VENUE	103
ALIEN ANT FARM	104
INFESTATION	105
WHAT THE	106
TURNING AWAY	107
FLAGRANT	108
CORRUPTION ERUPTION	109
LAWLESS ONES	110
SWITCHEROO	111

TWO-TIER	112
CRY WOLF	113
A GULAG PLOT	114
NOT YOU, THEN WHO	115
PARADISE PLUNDER	116
A FOWL PLAY	117
DEPLORABLE	120
COMMANDER AND THIEF	121
CITIZENS REIGN	122
LIES THE TRUTH	123
PROSPERITY AND POWER	124
DEATH OF DIALECTICS	125
NON-DISCLOSURE	126
ELITE DEFEAT	127
DECEPTION	128
SOVEREIGNTY	129
CHOOSE	130
MADNESS OF THE MASSES	131
MANIC	132
ABSOLUTE	133
WAKE UP	134
AWAKEN	135
UPSIDE DOWN WORLD	136
OXYMORON	137
BE VIGILANT	138
BE DILIGENT	139
NO LONGER BE	140
COLLATERAL CATTLE	141
AMONG US	142
SILENTLY SPEAKING	143
FREEDOM BE	144
CRIES OF DECEPTION	145
ABBA vs. ALLAH	146
REMEMBER SEPTEMBER	147
RECIPE FOR DISASTER	148
WARFARE'S MENU	149

FOOTSTEPS	150
FORTITUDE	151
INDEBTEDNESS	152
A SOLDIER'S GLORY	153
TO MY SON	154
THANK YOU LETTER	155
STAND UP	156
TRIBUTE	157
IN REMEMBRANCE	158
PRICE OF FREEDOM	159
THE HOMECOMING	160
CHRISTMAS LIST	161
FORGIVENESS	162
REMEMBER THEM	163
WE WILL STILL STRIVE	165
THE ULTIMATE SACRIFICE	166
BEYOND DUTY	168
EVENTUALLY	169
BEACON ON THE HILL	170
SO PROUD	171
ON THE HORIZON	172
NOTEWORTHY	173
SO THANKFUL	174
HOME COOKING	175
LAND OF THE GIVING	176
STAND TALL	177
THE CHOSEN	178
MONUMENTAL	179
HOME BLESSED	180
GRATITUDE	181
FREE AS A FISH	182
BEAUTIFUL, BEAUTIFUL	183
SKY HIGH	184
CLIMB TO THE TOP	185
MAKE MY WAY	186
BRAVE	187

THE BEST THERE IS	188
AMERICA	189
FREEDOM WITHIN	190
ROUNDABOUT	191
LIFE, LIBERTY LESSONS	192
SALUTE	193
ALLEGIANCE	194
ICONIC IMAGES	195
AMERICA STATE OF MIND	196

LIBERTY

One must fight for her honor to win her love.
For, she's a lady of virtue graced by God above.
And many have tried for her hand but failed.
When courting for her love but they're too frail.

Only those willing to die are strong to survive.
And win her heart the reward for freedom alive.
One must fight for her honor to win her love.
For, she is Lady Liberty graced by God above.

2023

UNITED STATES

We may be different, but we are the same.
For, we are united as one in this frame.
When, being a country, many of states.
That is the reason, why we're so great.
For, we are united as one in this frame.
We may be different, but we are the same.

2024

WE THE PEOPLE

We the people of the United States
Take back our country from those who break
Our sovereign laws when they don't care
About this nation and those who are there

We the people of the United States
Believe we are blessed to be a country great
And to share our good fortune those to be
One with, We the People together and free

2024

LONG LIVE LIBERTY

Since the beginning of our great nation freedom was at its core.
Many men and women who gave their lives opened up the door.
We must keep this door opened so other generations can be free.
If we allow this door to close, it will lead to the death of liberty.

For, surely we must stand together and keep our liberties strong.
No one has a right to take away what they feel we say, is wrong.
Our way of life, it has passed the test of time since it came to be.
A strong arm, will keep its door wide open, long live, our liberty.

2024

STARS AND STRIPES

The American flag is one of wonder, and pride.
For many men and women has fought and died.
When, they represented this great nation of ours.
It's symbol of our freedom since beginning hour.

The stars and stripes are not for decoration sake.
As there is meaning for their appearance to date.
Fifty stars represent, the fifty states, of this land.
And thirteen stripes are original colonies, grand.

The American flag is one of wonder, and pride.
For many men and women has fought and died.
When, they represented this great nation of ours.
It's symbol of our freedom since beginning hour.

2024

FOREVER FREE

We are born with a gift given at birth.
It is the air we breathe of life's worth.
No one can take this breath from you.
For, it is like wings of a bird that flew.
This is a one thing that will always be.
Just remember that you're forever free.

2023

LEARN TO FLY

Just as the eagle is the symbol of our freedom.
One must take that leap within to then become.
Free from those wishing to clip liberty's wings.
Let no one take away your eagle spirit to bring.
Even closer to your freedom you're like the sky.
When living in a democracy and learning to fly.

2024

EAGLE FREE

How dare one try to clip, my wings.
And silence my words, when I sing.
They've no power to control my life.

I'll fly like an eagle no one can stop.
My freedom to soar I stand at the top.
I will live my way, without their lies.

2024

EAGLE EYE

America is the eye, of an eagle that soars.
For, she keeps watch over a world's door.
When, many are like a predator to its prey.
She swoops to protect those without delay.
But even when she tries to do what's good.
She's just like an eagle and misunderstood.

2024

OUR BIRTHRIGHT

Freedom is not something one can give.
And legislate by law how one must live.
It is our, God given right, from the start.

From time we are born, we're to be free.
Our first breath of air is a moment to be.
Exactly like the eagle, with its free heart.

2024

THE FREE

We are the free like the world around me.
It is our birthright to be free like a bird.
And to soar with liberty our voices heard.

We are the free like the world around me.
It is our birthright to be free like a song.
And we sing our opinions not being wrong.

We are the free like the world around me.
It is our birthright to be free like a cloud.
And to have the freedom to travel allowed.

We are the free like the world around me.
It is our birthright to be free like the flag.
And wave our allegiance not afraid to brag.

2024

LIBERTY FREE

Our freedom is like, an eagle that flies.
That soars in the air with its sharp eyes.
With majestic wings, it glides by uplift.
Then powerful winds help, with its gift.

Of liberty to be the master of one's life.
To be as free as a bird, to be as you like.
No one has a right, take away, from me.
And be, like the eagle, to be liberty free.

2024

LET FREEDOM RING

I hear the bells ringing, it echoes in my ears.
I see a choir singing, there is nothing to fear.
I feel joy in knowing, liberty is a right to me.
I sense a day is coming, when we will be free.

2023

PATRIOTISM

A wave of the flag, or the salute, of a hand
Just a tiny gesture to express how we stand
To show to others in the pride that we share

For the love of our country to know we care
When many have died so that we can be free
Patriotism is not too much from you and me

2024

FREEDOM

Freedom is not free, it comes with a cost.

The many men and women lives are lost.

The sacrifice they've made is a gift to us.

Bought by their blood remember because.

The many men and women, lives are lost.

Freedom is not free, it comes with a cost.

2023

DIAMOND IN THE ROUGH

From America's beginning, it wasn't very clear.
This country's outcome, a poor condition feared.
For the British thought we're compared to devils.
And not thankful to the monarch we're but rebels.

Little did they realize how wrong they soon to be.
When, people are brought together, for its liberty.
But just like a diamond in the rough this outcome.
America a shining beacon valuable we've become.

2024

PATRIOT

Within the soul is deep love for this country.
It was those that fought and died we believe.
That laid, down their lives, so we can be free.

From the Revolutionary War, when it began.
To the present day freedom rings in this land.
And their unalienable rights woman and man.

2024

A CITIZEN TO BE
AND THE THREE COUNTRIES

Once upon a time, a long time ago,
there was a young explorer for a country to know.
He travelled far and wide on his way,
to discover a certain land we now live here today.

And first came upon a vast, coastal state,
when his initial impression was, this will be great.
But to his eye surprise it wasn't that way,
for this country was much too cold to its locals they.

As People's Republic were herded like sheep,
and ruled under a ruler without any liberties to keep.
So this one scout decided to continue to explore,
to discover a new discovery by knocking on its door.

He didn't need to travel what seemed very far,
because these two mass lands touched like the stars.
Again to his dismay, his eyes were deceived,
for this country was much too hot for him to believe.

As the proletariat they were treated as disease,
and kept to be depressed by their ruler that deceives.
Once again he explored to uncover a new land,
He vowed to discover a new land that will be grand.

A nation not too cold or too hot for people there,
but a place that's a welcome warmth and truly cares.
And then he came upon this land that is great,
for he discovered America, known as the United States.

When once upon a time, a long time ago,
there was a young explorer for a country to know.
He travelled far and wide on his way,
to discover a certain land we now live here today.

2024

SURVIVOR

Look back in history, to see, how we've strived.
From our beginning we shouldn't have survived.
When, we're nothing but minutemen that fought.
Against, perils of the English Army, who sought.

So we're not a sovereign nation home of the free.
It is our unalienable rights by God to you and me.
Look back in history, and see, how we've strived.
From our beginning, we shouldn't, have survived.

2024

CONSTRUCTION OF AMERICA

A myth is told of the perils of Valley Forge.
The harsh condition of winter was explored.
That caused a Continental Army to be weak.
But that was not the truth to a story we seek.

Valley Forge wasn't worst winter in this war.
There were also others only this came before.
Provisions of supplies could be procured then.
So George Washington had men build defend.

From the blistering cold log cabins were made.
Not only that but shoes and clothes that paved.
The way so well-equipped comrades could help.
In the construction of America they developed.

2023

OUR REPUBLIC

So you think we live in a democracy.
That's not quite right, but hypocracy.
We do have a say to voting outcome.
As that's one of our rights a freedom.

But our nation was set up, a republic.
Its forefathers had insight to develop.
A government represented each state.
Not just ones believing they are great.

2024

LIBERTY LIGHTS

"Son of the Republic, look and learn," was her cry.
For George Washington witnessed a lady close by.
The spirit extended her arm as a white vapor arose.
Then before him is countries of the world so it goes.

"Look and learn," said the voice, before him he saw.
A vision of villages, towns and cities sprung up tall.
Until he saw the image is filled between each ocean.
And this land will become a country was the notion.

"Son of the Republic, look and learn," she cried now.
A Crown of Light and "Union," appeared somehow.
Bearing the American Flag, as it flies high, the sight.
And believing this nation will be free was his might.

2023

LAND OF GIANTS

There are those that walked before us larger than life.
It's their legacy that made this nation's freedom alive.
And our forefathers brought forth a republic it's begun.
As first president of America was George Washington.

Years later a statesmen would come through the ranks.
A Kentucky lawyer was born within wilderness banks.
And proved he was a great president freeing the slaves.
Abraham Lincoln during the Civil War, America saves.

An American Christian minister raises his voice to stir.
He was a prominent activist and a political philosopher.
As a leader in the "Civil Rights" movement he believed.
When Martin Luther King Jr. cried out "I have a Dream."

But one president was a great politician and was an actor.
Ronald Reagan orders, "Tear down this wall" as a factor.
For, there are those that walked before us larger than life.
It's their legacy that has made this nation's freedom alive.

2024

CONSTITUTIONAL

We the people of the United States have designated rights.
It is supreme law we abide, for many have died, by a fight.
To supersede, Articles of Confederation, that came before.
A constitution balances national power in government lore.
The Constitution of the United States the frame of the land.
It constrains, federal authority, united we the people stand.

2024

LESSONS OF THE FREE

Speak your mind, don't be afraid to say
For freedom of speech is granted I pray

A right to bear arms, one able to defend
My freedom to live without fear I intend

To shelter soldiers without one's consent
A private citizen's home is not to be lent

Protection from the government is the act
Unreasonable searches and seizures a fact

The right for a criminal defendant to a trial
By unnecessary delays and a lawyer's style

It is conducted fairly and justly by a judge
That's impartial to a local without a grudge

2

Civil trials both the plaintiff and defendant
Has a constitutional right to a jury's verdict

Defendants have a right, released from jail
If one agrees to return to court after the bail

So individual natural rights everyone shares
Will be protected in the same way, as theirs

As political power held by each of the states
Rather than the federal government it makes

According to the Constitution in liberties be
Our unalienable rights are lessons of the free

2023

DECLARATION

Everyone at birth has a formal statement for life.
The day they are born they have God given rights.
No one is better and should be in front of the line.
We all start out naked it is our character this time.
That one should judge be not the color of our skin.
Look beyond for there're unique qualities to begin.
If everyone at birth has a formal statement for life.
Then the day one is born, one has God given rights.

2023

AMUCK

The right to freedom of speech is wildly out of control.
What gives, someone the right to silence anyone's soul.
Just because one believes, their ideas are the valid truth.
It doesn't mean in reality their truth, actually one's ruse.
If one is able to believe what they believe so should we.
Stop trying to cancel voices in a democracy we are free.

2023

VOICE OF FREEDOM

We are one voice the sound of freedom.
We are one choice, if we are, to become.
The nation our forefathers believed to be.
Of courage and valor, if we're to be free.
We stand together we cry with one voice.
We made a decision, freedom our choice.

2024

DON'T TREAD ON ME

Like approaching a snake one should keep their distance.
When, encroaching on my freedoms, a way of resistance.
The Declaration states to us God given inalienable rights.
And they're not to be stomped on or we'll stand and fight.
Liberty is a gift for us all, from our forefathers to this day.
So don't tread on me, if the ones who've died, have a say.

2023

FOREFATHERS' FRAME

How do we apologize to those from the past?
How can we when we are wearing this mask?

Do we just forget, all that they went through?
Do we lie and rewrite the red, white and blue?

Is it destiny for this country to deny the good?
Is it destiny for the people, forget what stood?

How can we not forgive, forefathers' shame?
How can we not be free a forefathers' frame?

2008

FRAMEWORK

To build, a house, one needs a strong frame
One that is sturdy and a country is the same
And holds it together, must be that of a rock
For the heart of lumber are a people of stock

Who, work to make the nation, strong for all
As they stand arm to arm, not letting her fall
To build a house, as needed is a strong frame
One that is sturdy and a country it's the same

2024

200 YEAR WARRANTY

How long has it been has it been centuries when?
Our forefathers chased a dream to build this place.
With pens they construct a constitution to conduct.
For tyranny will not ring freedom will be their king.
But how long has it been has it been centuries then?
Since a new world of grace was blessed to be great.
Alike the republics of lore, that arose but fell before.
There's no guarantee with only a 200 year warranty.

2008

DEATH OF A NATION

Are we on the path to destruction?
Are we blind not to see its construction?
Are we to let few determine a cost?
Are we so ignorant not to realize the lost?
Are we to let our history be, forgot?
Are we to say to ones who died it's for not?
Are we selfish to our children to be?
Are we denying new generations to be free?
Are we on a road to our elimination?
Are we no longer America death of a nation?

2023

AMERICA'S OBITUARY
July 4th 2023

It is with deep sorrow that our dear country has passed away.
She died July 4th, 2023, the age of 247 years old, her birthday.
A wonderful mother who was always there when needed help.
And she was very generous to all others even the less develop.
She had many of friends and was well-loved around the world.
For even those that tried to cause harm respected her emerged.
And many family members have passed away before her death.
Washington, Lincoln and King to name a few, a country's best.
Still those who survived, her untimely demise believe it would.
Be, a disservice to not continue her legacy of trying to do good.
So with broken hearts we come to announce the public funeral.
Of our great country, the United States of America, a memorial.

2023

BLINDSIDED

Better watch your back, when unable to see.
When, a punch is thrown by being deceived.
And told we're on your side they do convey.
But truth is they hope we look the other way.

It's in their actions that we should seek truth.
Not empty words, when they are only, a ruse.
Better watch your back, one being misguided.
When a punch is thrown as you're blindsided.

2024

PINOCCHIOBAMA

Once upon a time a father's political agenda
created a colorful, little puppet to someday become
president and named him PinocchiObama.
"How we wish PinocchiObama was a real president."
They kept saying to themselves.
"He would be our very own puppet."
One night while the American voter was sleeping,
the blue fairy brought the puppet to life.
The blue fairy spoke to PinocchiObama,
"You are still a puppet."
Then PinocchiObama's constitutional conscience said,
"But, if you are brave, truthful and unselfish, you will
become a real president."
PinocchiObama promised to do his best with
the help of The Constitution to guide
him along the way.
When the political agenda woke to find their
puppet was president, they danced with joy
at his inauguration.
But like all presidents, PinocchiObama went to Washington.
He hadn't gotten very far
when he met a sly fox of a man.
The man ran a puppet theatre and promised
to make PinocchiObama a star.
Everyone loved the puppet with his cute teleprompter.
PinocchiObama loved the bright lights and applause.
Then the American people confronted PinocchiObama,
"Why didn't you go to Washington and support us?"
"I....I was kidnapped by a blue monster!"
PinocchiObama lied. At that very moment,
his EGO grew bigger.
PinocchiObama told more lies, but the
American people still gave him another chance
with one condition. "You must do what is
good and right." With that his EGO grew smaller.

2

Once again PinocchiObama headed straight for Washington. On the way he met an evil madam. The madam offered to take PinocchiObama to congress.
"Don't go with her!" pleaded The Constitution.
But, PinocchiObama jumped on the band wagon driven by a sad team of jackasses and off he went.
Congress was a wondrous place. PinocchiObama could do whatever he wanted because there were no grown-ups to stop him.
But then PinocchiObama realized something amazing was happening to him while manipulating congress. He was growing jackass ears and a crooked tail. Soon he would be nothing but a jackass pulling the madam's agenda.
The Constitution spoke to PinocchiObama,
"To escape the jackass held congress, you must listen to the American people and not stay with your political roots."
But PinocchiObama was swallowed up by his whale of lies.
"This is not my fault," cried PinocchiObama.
"I am their puppet."
In no time PinocchiObama's true nature was exposed.
And his political followers cried,
"PinocchiObama is this the real you and are these jackass ears for real?" Together they schemed a plan of escape using smoke and mirrors.
Will the American people see through the smoke and mirrors and hold PinocchiObama Accountable to The Constitution?
Will PinocchiObama become brave, truthful and unselfish?
Will his lies and EGO grow smaller?
Will The Constitution prevail?
How will President PinocchiObama's story end?
Will it be in LIBERTY or TYRANNY?

2009

ROOTED

Deep within one's being is a majestic tree.
It's where we branch out and become free.
Steadfast in the beliefs we come to believe.
They're our core values no one can deceive.
And take away what is rooted in one's soul.
By chopping to stop and try to take control.

2022

DEFIANCE

Our country's roots are deep seeded.
When, patriots did what was needed.
And create a nation with civil liberty.
Of God given rights our freedom, be.

Not taken for granted by all we share.
Our gift wrapped by their blood there.
From the rebellion there's rule of law.
As history, repeats itself when we fall.

2023

A CIVIL CRY

A civil cry can be heard bellowing from this bane land
For the Delta lies scarred amid specter ruins buried deep
Within scarlet clay abut by blood stained tears that weep
By the combatants engaged to goad their oppugned stand

The North evolved and is a territory suitable for industry
But, the South, preserved a culture to cultivate the loam
In the politics of bondage, retained their ancestral home
To omit progression of exemption Northward did believe

In a country divided hence The War Between the States
There a crusade is rivalry by contention as a cry of strife
Be each side, pledged allegiance to uphold a way of life
For brothers fought against brothers a battle not to delay

In the outset of war the South levied to forfend its realm
For it was not required to conquer the North to succeed
As a duty to defend a way of life, they unduly believed
And thus unaware, the Union's myriad of armor stealth

2

Hosts of men were dying, slaughtered upon the environment
This tally of troops suffered severely among wars bitter cold
For civil warfare conceived an entity indigenous to take hold
And the soldiers were ill equipped to battle man and elements

With a shudder of drums an emissary foretells a peril by beat
The manifold of sufferers are victims mutilated beyond lame
As countless array of bodies are abandoned by death's game
For the sake of honor is its country's blood, spilt upon defeat

An enigma no longer kept from the race of this vast mold
That a war among its own people is a greater toll for harm
Then a war fought against people far away, executing alarm
It is a lesson never to be forgotten, a tale forever to behold

Let not this fountainhead of civil diversity be put to shame
By remembering the genesis of one's equal right by demise
A civil cry can be heard upholding the battle for justice arise
For brothers fought against brothers, they did not die in vain

2003

AUTARKY

As a nation we have fought and died for liberty.
From the beginning we've had, self sufficiency.
We have God given rights and autonomy to live.
Not be ruled by a dictator but self govern to give.
An opportunity is the ability to control one's life.
As a nation we march to a different drum and fife.

2024

TWIST OF FATE

A cold wind blew within a camp, molesting combatants at sleep
As bleached tents grazed the hillside, resembling a herd of sheep
A regiment awaited warfare for days, null upon the guardian hill
For Union troops abide to this slaughtering, or be as prey killed
There, dying embers afloat mid camp, imitates fireflies at dance
Lays the assemblage of men, believed a battle soon to be at hand

A certain soldier arose mid frigid sleep unable to contain his fear
Recall the rhythmic beating of drums announcing the enemy near
Nearby the Confederates' encampment shelters the adjacent loam
The lanky lad perched uncertain haunted by memories from home
For a sibling remembered flogging drums similar to the eerie beat
He's aware of the inevitable contact by opposing warriors to meet

2

The early morning embarked while officers corralled men in lines
Be the levy in front to kneel down as a series in back stood behind
A stretch of blue wool across the terrain befits a barbed-wire fence
As a dull beating of drums rumbled for the battle was to commence
In rows of dye, marching up the hill, a gray fog rolled up the knoll
Then smoke from fire intertwines with sums defeated by death's toll

The hue of blue and gray bleeds mid haze behooved by war's ware
By guns discharging demise, so that both sides refute God's stare
A command to impede firing is declared to all who have survived
For a cheering mob, embrace a deity's virtue of fortune to be alive
A sibling recalled in a sea of blood for a souvenir to be recovered
As a twist of fate, befalls upon by stealing the drum off his brother

2003

GHOSTLY GROUNDS

Where those that have fought and died.
The wind still carries their solemn, cry.
Across its blood stain fields from battle.
For death lives on, when lives are cattle.
And forgotten like its windswept sound.
From one's howls from ghostly grounds.

2024

SACRED SOIL

For those that have died and paid the price.
A resting place must be their home, suffice.
Where one's tormented soul can be at peace.
As they've done their duty, by their decease.
It's with courage they no longer need to toil.
They paid a price to be buried on sacred soil.

2024

PAID IN FULL

The debt has been paid long before your birth.
Not by any currency but by a life's worth.
Of countless men who gave their lives in blood.
That bled on the battlefield covered in mud.
And now you say it's not enough men who died.
You want retributions with money it's cried.
But the debt has been paid long before your birth.
Not by any banks but in full by a life's worth.

2023

DEBT FREE

The past is the past and is there to remind us.
Of lessons learnt, the future, will not find us.
If we make, same mistakes, as we did before.
But that doesn't mean we must pay to restore.
What was done long ago we should not judge.
And think we are better, by holding, a grudge.
The past is the past to learn from but let it be.
As a part of our history paid, we are debt free.

2024

HUMBLE PIE

Mistakes were made yesterday and today.
Our country is not perfect, that is our say.
But at least we try to make the best to be.
A nation of civil rights, created to be free.

History isn't perfect or the future beyond.
We will make mistakes we need to go on.
And swallow pride not seeing, eye to eye.
There's a lesson learnt, eating humble pie.

2024

WALK THROUGH TIME

Take me back, to yesteryear when all I hear are your fears.
Don't you, realize, that a lot of your cries, nothing but lies.
A walk through time maybe it is to find you are out of line.
History made yes some misbehaved, but many were saved.
Take a look what it took for our forefathers to write a hook.
For us all to be free, not just you and me, but entire country.

2024

LIVE AND LEARN

Life is a series of classes along the way.
Some are hard knocks some will make your day.
Either way it is to teach you how to live.
Nothing comes by easy, when living like a sieve.
One must take the punches, to then, earn.
Your place in a democratic society, live and learn.

2024

HISTORY'S LESSON

The past is a great reminder for the present known.
If only we'd remember what its yesteryear shown.
Then maybe, we would learn from a mistake made.
And correct the error before another one is obeyed.
For we attend the school of life, must pay attention.
So we can amend the future from a history's lesson.

2023

EVOLUTION OF WAR

A shrill cry echoes within the jungle of man's ancestry.
The screeching sound is feared amid the lush greenery.
This scenery will protect them with nature's umbrellas.
It is a safe haven from scorching heat and pouring rain.
But, there's nothing to stop what lurks within the trees.

In alarm they pace the forest floor and fly among vines.
They are nervous with nowhere to hide from the danger.
As there, will be destruction in war among them selves.
There's no villain when all are victims to Mother Nature.
But, there will be a massacre by virility within the trees.

Aggression will intimidate, using branches for weapons.
With arms high to appear enormous they attack the weak.
There is no mercy granted, they gnaw off hands and feet.
And a shrill cry echoes within a jungle of man's ancestry.
But, there is nothing to stop its evolution within the trees.

2009

WHY

Like, father
Like, son
Why, bother
Death will come

Like, cattle
To the slaughter
Why, bother
Hatred's won

Like, history
Through the ages
Why, bother
War's begun

Like, father
Like, son
Why, bother
Death will come

2008

HUMAN WALL

Each man is a fence, tainted with his greed
Wired, stoned, wooded in the seed
Inherited by blood to all
Mayhem is painted upon the human wall
The paint is prejudice
Its torch was to burn into my no longer flesh
No God spewed fury bellowing from the hills
I was not to die on this cross, I am their will
My body nailed to bodies on each side
Their motive no longer can hide
I was to be baptized
Paint was brushed into my eyes
The distemper burned as it gave me light
Man in duress captured my sight
Paint was brushed into my ears
The distemper burned as I began to hear
I was to hear prejudice my first word
Taught exactly the way the sound should
Paint was brushed onto my tongue
The distemper burned as animosity begun
I saw myself begin to shout
Taunting and jeering with flout
Paint was brushed onto my hands
The distemper burned as fetter demands
I saw myself repressing man
I have done what they command
Within throe prejudice weighed me off the cross
I felt the nails become loose and lost
I fell from the fog and gloom
Born from my mother's womb
Not wired, stoned, wooded, I am flesh
I will not hold my brother's hand in prejudice
A blemish upon the human wall
Never mended each fence will demise and fall

1975

SILENCE SPEAKS

Saying nothing speaks louder than words.
Having no opinion is thought undisturbed.
When, floating downstream with the flow.
The world passes you by, not in the know.

Jump into the water go against its current.
Say what is on your mind, not afraid of it.
Having no opinion is thought undisturbed.
Saying nothing, speaks louder than words.

2023

FREEDOM'S DECREE

Lady Liberty's there to demand.

Her freedom's to be across our land.

From the many brave whose lives lost.

In wars they have fought and paid the cost.

So their children may have the right to be free.

By Lady Liberty as she stands for freedom's decree.

2023

CALL OF THE FREE

A rebel yell is heard throughout the land.
For, liberty is a right to woman, and man.
No one is the better and can control those.
That they deem lesser in value, so it goes.
But we have one voice, stand up for right.
If they think they'll take it away, we fight.
And justice will be on our side in the end.
The call of the free can be there to defend.

2024

WILDERNESS WITHIN

The call of the free is within you and me
The wilderness within, is a cry to be free
We are among, the patriots from our past
When, taking up arms for freedom at last

The birth of a nation, fought among trees
That is where minutemen came to be free
With God and Mother Nature by our side
Where a wilderness within has never died

2024

FEARLESS

Just like the wolf one must be.
Fearless if they wish to be free.
In a wilderness they try to run.
From its traps of those become.

To be caught in mindless cage.
And all they feel is hate's rage.
Just like the wolf, one must be.
Fearless if they wish to be free.

2024

CRY OF THE FREE

It is the same in the wild as it is in the tame.
A sound may be different not one's exclaim.
The shrill of one's voice will let all to know.
Like a wolf in the forest, that howls to show.
No one can take away my freedom to be me.
And to live with liberty is the cry of the free.

2023

LIBERTY'S SPOKEN

She is calling out across the land
A majestic weeping willow stand
Her tears for alarm befall on man
Wake up, get up, liberty's spoken

America, be on the alert and band
Together we can win and demand
For freedom what makes us grand
Will never, ever be, liberty broken

She is calling out across the land
A majestic weeping willow stand
Her tears for alarm befall on man
Wake up, get up, liberty's spoken

2007

LIBERTY BROKEN

She is crying for us, across, this land.
Her cry is for all and to make a stand.
Before it's too late, she is just a token.
America's a memory liberty is broken.

2024

UNITED WE STAND

Together we can make a difference if we try.
We are one body on this journey live and die.
There's no reason go against the other's trust.
Everyone has the right to say what they must.
For, that is what was to be the law of the land.
We may be different, but it's, united we stand.

2024

DIVIDED WE FALL

Just because we're different we can't try.
To be as one body this journey flying by.
What, reasons are there to go against trust.
If everyone has the right to say they must.
That is what should be, the law, for us all.
When, we can't be as one, divided we fall.

2024

LIVE AND LET BE

Don't tread on me for what I believe.
I have rights to my opinions you see.
Just like you, my life, it's my choice.
If I don't talk like you, it's my voice.

I wouldn't tell you what you can say.
So stop telling me I must speak a way.
That goes against all that I do believe.
Just live your life, but, let me, just be.

2023

DREAM ON

Reality is a ruse
No longer is a truth
In the world today

So I'll dream away
A world I wish to be
Where I can be free

2024

MY CHOICE

I choose to be free.

I choose to be me.

I choose to let be.

I choose liberty.

I choose to live.

I choose to give.

I choose to forgive.

I choose to relive.

I choose to believe.

I choose to grieve.

I choose to receive.

I choose to achieve.

I choose to be free.

I choose to be me.

I choose to let be.

I choose liberty.

2024

LET ME BE

No one has the right, to tell me what to think.
I have my opinions and that's freedom's link.
To the many blessings we share with this land.

So that is why we honor her and make a stand.
For, she was built by our blood to keep us free.
No one has the right to take that away from me.

2023

ONE ARE WE

As individuals we are a country one.
Together, we make this body begun.
And stand up, for rights of everyone.
So no one takes away one's freedom.

To those who speak their mind freely.
It is their right to agree or to disagree.
And be the children of a Lady Liberty.
For we are still united but one, are we.

2024

OWNERSHIP

This is your country just as much as theirs.
Don't let them fool you for they don't care.
We must take back as citizens, given rights.
For no one is better than the other in might.
They may try to change the rules, interpret.
But we know for a fact we have ownership.

2023

WE ARE ONE

United we are for our country we.
We are one body but individually.
Together we stand for rights of all.
So no one can take away their call.

And speak their mind they believe.
Is their right from our Lady Liberty.
And be in agreement for we've won.
To still be united but yet we are one.

2023

TO BE HONEST

I for one believe in this country so great.
The men and women who have what it takes.
But as we don't believe, it won't take very long.
To be honest I'm afraid, our freedoms will be gone.

2024

HONESTY

I honestly cannot tell what is the truth.
When, both sides are telling me, a ruse.
Do they, truly believe we believe its lie.
We're beneath them but they're up high.

I honestly don't care how they think so.
When, they are the ones, sinking so low.
Do they, wish for humanity, to go away.
We're here to stay, that I'll honestly say.

2024

CRIES OF LIES

I have heard their lies from both sides now
Democrat or a Republican doesn't matter somehow
When most of them are in it for themselves
They leave the public service, serving only for itself
I'm tired being told they are for the good
Stop the deceiving cries saying you're misunderstood
We elected you for one purpose and that be
To serve the American people for our freedom's liberty

2024

BURRO BUREAUCRACY
The Democratic Party
(Political Poetry I)

Take heed party of munificent deeds
Regard the ability of mankind's seeds
Endowing fish amid the crying of yearn
Believing the multitude, unable to learn
Your belief in the bounded duty to feed
Man's conclusion, absent of arms indeed
Conceive to deceive the populous political
By reaping one's hungriness as analytical
Rise and edify the desire to assist oneself
Health in humanity, one who helps himself

2003

ZOMBIES vs. VAMPIRES
Democrats vs. Republicans

Lifeless eyes
Moaning cries
Dead men walk
Same ole talk
All they care
Everyone share
In the disease
As zombies

Piercing fangs
In the game
At the top
Blood drops
All may try
Some will die
In the empire
As vampires

2012

PACHYDERM POLITICS
The Republican Party
(Political Poetry II)

Take heed party of immutable creeds
Regard the appetite of mankind's needs
To indoctrinate a man where with to fish
An absence of hunger, a hypocrisy wish
Wait, what if the man is absent of arms
Naught entitled to fulfill voracity's harm
Autonomy alone won't feed a man's pride
Compassion of self, humanity must abide
Teach knowledge to a man able proficient
Bestow servitude to persons less sufficient

2003

RIGHTEOUSNESS

We as a nation must live up to our might.
If we to be in favor to be good and right.
There's a duty to be in grace and blessed.
For, we shall be among the righteousness.

2024

STATUE OF FREEDOM

She holds a sword within her hand.
The Roman goddess of war makes a stand.
For, she defends the temple gates of Rome.
She is the sister of Mars as she is known.
And wears a military helmet upon her head.
In the name of bravery for she has bled.
The Statue of Freedom on the Capital's dome.
She protects the United States, her new home.

2020

MILITARY MIGHT

It is with strength we are able to thrive.
And be the nation that we are to survive.
So we carry a big stick it is in full sight.
Those wish us harm, our military might.

2024

COURAGE

One never knows if they possess this gift.
Until the time one is face to face with it.
Whether you run in fear, or stand to see.
There's part of oneself that is able to be.
As brave as a lion you're up against fear.
But, something's inside, you'll find near.
One never knows if they possess this gift.
Until the time its call of bravery is swift.

2023

MY DAD

Before I was born
His story was there
About a brave, young man
I wish to share

The years of his youth
In lessons he found
Were not from a book
But, from his small town

And the guidance he knew
From his parents' strong
Even when he's away to war
Back home is where he belongs

With the love of his life
And their children four
He works hard for them all
That's what a father is for

Before I was born
His story I am so glad
About a brave, young man
I'm proud to call my dad

2023

KNEW HE MUST GO

He heard the whistle, knew he must go
This train of his took him to war
Gripping his bag all he had to show
His mind wondering what the fighting was for

He heard the explosion, knew he must go
The war he's in took him to die
Gripping his life all he had to show
His mind asking the question why

He heard the bugle, knew he must go
That train to war is now in the past
Gripping his God all he had to show
Was his life worth it, he did ask

1975

SLOGORN

A rallying cry can be heard, across the land.
It's our battle cry of the republic to make a stand.
For, what is right and just, is good for us all.

That is why we must come together to say its call.
Unlike the Highland hosts an army of the dead.
We are the United States and our slogan to be said.

2024

THE DIE CRY

From the graves our military lie.
Can be heard their battle cry.
We have fought to save the free.
Let not our freedom die it be.

The cost we paid for liberty here.
We gave our lives do not fear.
From the graves, our military lie.
Can be heard, their battle, cry.

2024

BEAUTY BLOOMED

The landscapes of the First World War were once barren.
With the bodies of its soldiers maimed and killed there in.
From artillery shells, that dug and burnt the soil in its lust.
Will, their lives ever be remembered as they lie in the dust.

For the scarred land from bombing, would not ever forget.
Lost souls on the battlefield where their life and death met.
So began a proliferation growth of its dormant poppy seeds.
It's a symbol of the sacrifice of each soldier in war who bleed.

2023

POPPY

Red are the petals of this beautiful, flowering plant.
For its story has span the time throughout ages past.
By ancient Egyptian warriors fought to win its spell.
And addicted veterans of a Civil War do, tell it well.

But, the most amazing tale comes from a battlefield.
There soldiers who fought in a World War revealed.
The blitzed, barren land paid homage to men fought.
By a colorful, red flower that grew amid death's lot.

2023

OPERATION DETACHMENT

During World War II, there were many battles fought.
But one specifically mentioned within a history's plot.
The United States Navy and the Marine Corps is there.
To capture Iwo Jima Island from Japanese Army's lair.

Control of two airfields in the Pacific Japan possessed.
South Field and Central Field was an operation contest.
But some did not believe capturing the island was right.
In a decision to win against the Imperial Japanese fight.

For the enemy held positions the island's fortified great.
With a dense network of bunkers tunnels they did make.
The American, ground forces were supported to the hilt.
From naval artillery and help from the Marines but still.

A battle was fought for five-weeks few prisoners taken.
Many Japanese soldiers were killed their lives forsaken.
Not the American solider, by a photograph, taken there.
Six Marines raise the U.S flag top of a mount with care.

2023

RED, WHITE AND BLUE

If we do not know, what the colors, of the flag stand for.
Then, how can we expect anyone, to respect her for sure.
To some she's nothing but a piece of cloth nothing more.
And to others she's just flag that is flown but then stored.

She is much more than what appears flapping in the wind.
The red symbolizes hardiness and valor a country to begin.
And the white is a symbol for purity, and innocence a call.
The blue represents vigilance, perseverance, justice for all.

So that is why we should honor and respect her is in deed.
For men and women who've paid the price they did bleed.
Who fought, died for this great country we hold to be true.
And that is why we need to respect the red, white and blue.

2024

MEDAL OF HONOR

To those who are guardians of this great nation of ours.
And serve the United States Armed Forces, they tower.
With conspicuous gallantry one performs beyond a call.
At the risk of their own life they will disregard any fall.
For their intrepid actions they to be recognized by name.
The President, issues the Medal of Honor, with acclaim.

2024

BEYOND BRAVERY

Up on a cliff where a battle took place.
There many to meet death face to face.
For enemy troops waited them to come.
To climb the ridge, the fight has begun.

The Battle of Okinawa, the last of it be.
It's final battle World War II in history.
Both sides bore heavy losses in its fight.
As artillery fire explodes day and night.

But a young private save many of lives.
Who, are caught in a cross-fire derived.
So he carries wounded right on his back.
And applies bandages of hope they lack.

But even though, he is also injured there.
He continues to help others with his care.
He's awarded Medal of Honor, gallantry.
Beyond, call of duty, it is for his bravery.

2023

ABOUT FACE

One should stand at attention, honoring the flag.
It's not to be boastful to all the others or to brag.
But honor men and women who fought and died.
Because of their bravery we're on freedom's side.
So think twice before disrespecting a flag in haste.
Remember what it stands for, so do an about-face.

2023

PRISONER OF WAR

The tree was my home swaying in the air
Praying to be reborn as its fruit
Wanting to be apart of its life

In the shuffling of leaves appeared my
Enemies crawling on their bellies
Hissing sounds penetrated in my mind
As their fangs gripped into my flesh
Tearing me away
I fell as an apple from its mother tree

I was dragged by their ropes
Commanded to walk from their tongues
Giving only jargon
They led me to hell to be tortured by
The devil
His fire of propaganda belched from
His foaming mouth destroying my mind

2

He took away my soul
Thrown in a box to become his fruit
Coming out only to be eaten until I
Was nothing but a core

Their deviled tails wrapped around
My naked body controlling the very
Air I breathed
My existence was clandestine
If they had wished my life could
Have been dropped in the waste
Forgotten

1975
Dedicated to a military pilot
Who spoke at my school
Washington High, Sioux Falls, SD
I do not remember his name
But I will never forget his story

LEFT TO ONESELF

Alone, he stands on a street corner.
There uphold premises as a sojourner.
His hand stretched out toward the street.
Signals, his silent cry for something to eat.
Homeless man carries a world on his back.
Everything owned in the duffle bag packed.
And a beat-up guitar held across the shoulder.
To keep demons at bay, for a Nam-vet soldier.
Wanton ways replaced a future of any wealth.
Society abandoned a son to be left to oneself.

2004

UP IN ARMS

Silent, black-eyes protrude from his seclusion, peeping with amazement at the carnival-like atmosphere of his country. His dark, glassy-jewels are worthless; even though they imitate diamonds dancing in a river. The bewildered boy's hair simulates the rich darkness of night. Strands of hair crawl across his forehead in a snake-like motion. Tiny, yellowish hands swish back straggles to partake in the departure from his home. He is a war orphan. Placed in the arms of a soldier, he bounces like a woman's breast as they scurry towards the impending airplane. They reach their destination and he is raised to unknown arms.

A gentle breeze transports the sheerness of her robe and enshrouds his body. Together, they travel through a mirror of clouds. The mushroom skyscrapers constructed by the war's bombing in Vietnam are now transposed to skyscrapers in a concrete forest. The air pollution of death and decay become an irritating pollen in the air. The timid boy, blinks and rubs his eyes in wonder. They entered into a wonderland; America, his new home. The enchanted boy is mesmerized.

The reputed apparition is the Figure of Justice. She is wearing a blindfold resembling a crown of thorns. The timorous boy whispers a woeful whimper. It is a cry a puppy whines after being torn from its mother, only to be cast into a dark box. She holds his face into her hands. The cup of her hands brings his tears to her lips. Her smile embraces his soul. The placid boy was no longer in a cage with fear. He smiles the width of a puppy's tail; wagging with content. They are now able to communicate, empowering communion.

2

He points to the blindfold. Her auburn hair and robe are blowing in the wind like the American flag, but he has an uneasy feeling a blindfold means not wanting to see the truth.

"Why do you cover your eyes?" She touches the symbolic cloth that is caging her eyes. "I have taken your soul, the soul of a war orphan to teach him the symbols of his new home.

It is my gift to you." She holds his hand and points to a statue. "This is the Statue of Liberty, a symbol of hope for the homeless. She is a bosom of milk for all immigrants. She burns a mother's love in the torch that represents the fire for life."

The Statue of Liberty turns her face away from him. The grieved boy glowers at the apparition. She did not notice the statue rejecting her newborn. The cursed boy sees vessels transporting the outcast to this wonderland; only to be exiled by their new home. He felt betrayed. The apparition raised her arms in praise. "The fire for life will forever burn in the torch the statue upholds." The flame was not burning.

She holds his hand and points to a bell. He traces the crack in the bell with his finger. It imitates a mouse scurrying though a maze. He glares at the apparition. Her arms were raised in praise, unable to detect his puzzlement. "This is the Liberty Bell. It is the symbol of our independence. It rings for freedom and is heard throughout the world. It is ringing now." The conflicted boy touches the exposed crack. Within the fracture flows a trickle of blood. The bell was dying. Liberty was not ringing from its dome. He heard deceit clanging everywhere. The crack becomes a street consumed with rioting, refuting hope for the homeless.

3

She holds his hand and points to a gavel. An appendage appears from a black shadow pounding the gavel. It echoes somber, bashing sounds. The apparition raised her arms in praise." The gavel is the symbol of orderliness. It is used to enforce order in the courtrooms." The dolorous boy pries at the apparition. She is blind to what is actually befalling beyond the gavel. A baton held in the hands of a law officer, imitates dull, thumping sounds. The apparition did not notice the bludgeon splitting heads. "The gavel is a peaceful, civilized tool to enforce order."

She holds his hand and touches the symbolic cloth caging her eyes. He feels the thorns of her crown. "I am the Figure of Justice. I wear the blindfold to free myself from prejudice. I am the symbol for equality." The addled boy peers at the apparition. Her arms were raised in praise. He could not comprehend the reality of her crest. The blindfold resembled a wallet encased with dollar bills exposing an uncovered eye. "Everyone deserves equal justice." The apparition appeased gathers the trivial boy. "Our journey has been fulfilled."

Hand in hand they transcend to a descending plane. A faint breeze transports the sheerness of her robe and enshrouds his body. His soul enters a sleepy, little boy cuddling the warmth of an airplane seat. The plane lands in America, his new home. The divested boy, held in a fetal position, is lowered into unknown arms.

1976

CRY OF INNOCENCE

Blitz of bullets take their toll.
Silence cries its haunting roll.
Across the torrid land it takes.
Those forgotten those forsake.
It's in mankind's hell they die.
A song of innocence is the cry.
Child in time the war will take.
A death will be their only sake.

2023

DEVIL DEVIL

cold to a crisp
stroking hands shiver in mist
glittering eyes stare upon
hunger pains carry him on

mercy lord his wounds have bled
poverty stricken parents dead
stumbling the ruins of his town
searching warmth none is found

as howling sounds crawl from under
small hands cover the shriek of thunder
lights of heat surround his home
crying to be heard although alone

devil devil you are cold
you are war i am told
devil devil leave me alone
you are evil you are stone

tattered body lies in tears
no more sounds no more fears
cold no longer shivers his hand
he will not learn the devil was man

1975

WARFARE'S VENUE

ANALYSIS
NOT
TRAINABLE
SPECIES

2007

ALIEN ANT FARM

I look around staring, and what do I see.
We're all in a straight line, waiting to be.
Marching, marching, we are robotic ants.
Mindless like insignificant insects prance.
Going deep into holes we forgo the alarm.
But it's only an illusion in reality its harm.
Humanity will devour itself no one is safe.
We're all aliens as there is no secure place.

2023

INFESTATION

They are coming in swarms when entering here.
And soon they'll devour, what we hold, so dear.
Liken locust that consume vast acreages of land.
This is the United States so we must take a stand.

We welcome those that wish to be, and blend in.
And is apart of our society, with talents to begin.
They celebrate their new life with blessings here.
Not trying to destroy, our way of life, we do fear.

2024

WHAT THE

What the heck is going on?
When all around me is going wrong!

2023

TURNING AWAY

One must look straight ahead and not turn away.
From what is happening, to our freedoms, today.
Do not be blinded, by their shiny promises, said.
By turning away and not realizing we will be led.
We're down a wrong path and liberty gone astray.
If we're not being careful, not alert, turning away.

2024

FLAGRANT

It's a shame when one dishonors the American flag.
For, it is stitched with blood of those that didn't lag.
And stayed behind, when one's freedom cries a call.
They were first in line to sign up and fight for us all.

It may be your right to disrespect what it stands for.
Just remember, ones who died, opened up this door.
That allow you to have the liberty to shout and rant.
But it's in spirit of the American flag lives did grant.

2024

CORRUPTION ERUPTION

It seems like an atomic bomb, has been deployed
There's an explosion of violence, hate with noise
No one is safe from the spew of destructed malice
Why can't we act like adults, stop all the madness
Before this warhead we created, by our corruption
Will destroy everything that's good by its eruption

2024

LAWLESS ONES

There are those who cry wolf just to do so.
As they like to disrupt the order that we go.
For it's in their interest in a society corrupt.
It is then they can go about a sinfulness rot.
But we must call them out before it's begun.
And take back our nation from lawless ones.

2023

SWITCHEROO

Imagine this world of ours balanced and fair.
With its people compensated for their right share.
For knowledge passed on to each generation.
Will give teachers star quality of manifestation.
And to those on the battlefield by lives lost.
Give the soldiers ability to negotiate any cost.
Imagine this world of ours balanced and fair.
With its people compensated for their right share.
For fantasy on stage and movies they're upon.
Will give entertainers a teacher's meager income.
And the players on teams fans have watched.
Receive a soldier's pay which is not that much.
Imagine this world of ours balanced and fair.
With its people compensated for their right share.

2004

TWO-TIER

Some seem to tip the scale, when it comes to Lady Liberty.

They use the power of the purse, and their status to be free.

When all others are judged by the crimes they may commit.

Not the elite getting a free pass for they're better they admit.

Their day of judgment is to come it's not when they are here.

And die like the rest of us so heaven and hell is also two-tier.

2024

CRY WOLF

Be alarmed, when you hear, you should not fear.
From those in charge with large teeth come near.
And proclaim they are here, to help all the sheep.
Those they see grazing so free without their keep.
It is they who wish to control everything you do.
They come as good shepherds, if only you knew.
What's actually underneath the skin reveals a lie.
A howl from a wolf in sheep's clothing is the cry.

2023

A GULAG PLOT

RESTITUTION

It all began within a plot of land. And on this land lived many sheep.
When sheep before owned sod worth grand but many more dirt cheap.
Those who had nothing to show, not even a piece of grass they owned.
Did work the land so sod would grow, their measly pay is profits sown.
And that is why the story lies between those who have and those do not.
As those who do not begin to cry, demanding they deserve their fair lot.

REVOLUTION

Their cries are heard throughout the land, for wolf ears pick up the scent.
The pack comes up with a grand plan. They call for a rebellion or repent.
They promise the workers equal pay but did not disclose the hidden truth.
That equality meant freedom astray, but reality wolves will rule the roost.
And so the sheep took up arms, with the wolves, an uprising came about.
When soon they were alarmed for this is not what we want they did shout.

RESOLUTION

"Too late", the wolves howled. And the sheep were sent to prisons to pay.
For no one is allowed to scowl. If you do, they're ways to make you obey.
But, not all the sheep will bow down, to the wolves that have plenty to eat.
Some would rather drown then be on the wolves' dinner plate as their meat.
Just remember it is never greener on the other side, freedom is always best.
"Every sheep is unique" they cried, we will not follow the herd like the rest.

2020

NOT YOU, THEN WHO

If all you do is complain, and not even try.
To be apart of the solution as one they rely.
On, it takes courage to stand up against all.
Who, believe in only themselves, their call.
And hurt the ones that try to stop evil ways.
If, not you then who to fight for better days.

2023

PARADISE PLUNDER

Our lives will soon rot not from the outside but within
For, our world will be forgot, if we don't start to begin
And clean up our act by taking care of what is our own
That means citizens for a fact, not all others that grown
In numbers, they cross our borders, as if there is no law
To stop their crossing when it's we are the ones to crawl
We're begging please stop our paradise from going under
As our world will be forgot, if we don't stop this plunder

2023

A FOWL PLAY
(A Foul Play)

THE CAST

Benjamin .... Turkey 1
Franklin .... Turkey 2
Paul... Turkey 3
Revere .... Turkey 4
The Farm .... Remaining Turkeys
The White Cloaks .... Islamic Oppression

SETTING

The curtain opens to the setting of a turkey farm in a rural community within the United States. There are hundreds of gobbling, white fowl kneeling toward the East. The brown dirt resembles a web of blankets.

ACT ONE

Turkey 1 is leaning over, trying not to be noticed, to speak to turkey 2.

BENJAMIN: We keep praying and praying to their god. Has it done us any, good?

FRANKLIN: You still have your neck, don't you?

BENJAMIN: But, not my freedom, as for my neck, it is still in their noose and at any given moment my neck will end up just like my freedom, choked.

FRANKLIN: So, what do you have up your wing?

BENJAMIN: We, turkeys need to have a revolution and take back this farm. The bald eagle may be the symbol for freedom, but, we were the first in line.

FRANKLIN: You're right. Who decided on the eagle, anyway? We're ones who gave their necks for this country. If, I'm gonna die. I'm gonna die, free.

BENJAMIN & FRANKLIN: (Simultaneously) FREEDOM!

(THE CURTAIN CLOSES)

ACT TWO

The curtain opens to the sight of many dead fowl spewed across the terrain. Turkey 3 and turkey 4 are discussing amongst themselves, a plan of action.

PAUL: They didn't even see it coming. One turkey looks up in the rain, and before you know it, they're all, looking up and for what? A young turkey is told he'll go to heaven if he looks up and kills himself and countless others.

REVERE: There's talk through the fowl vine of a revolt. A revolution.

PAUL: Yeah, I heard. We can't live like this anymore, not knowing which day to the next when they will cut our throats. At least, under a democracy our hearts were free.

REVERE: Give me freedom, or cut my neck!!!

PAUL: Not so loud, we need our necks for this revolution.

REVERE: Well sir, start sticking your neck out because the revolt is to begin.

PAUL & REVERE: (Simultaneously) The White Cloaks are coming! The White Cloaks are coming!

(THE CURTAIN CLOSES)

As Paul & Revere start a revolt with wings flapping and feet mapping.

ACT THREE

The white cloaks, and Islamic oppression are crushed to death by the farm with its remaining turkeys. The curtain opens to the setting of a turkey farm in a rural community within the United States. There are hundreds of gobbling, white fowl kneeling and looking toward the heavens. Giving thanks to God and for freedom.

(THE CURTAIN CLOSES)

2008

DEPLORABLE

One should look in the mirror when they convey.
We are among the deplorable that she did say.
As if, you can so judge someone, like hysterical.
We may be, deplorable, but you are pathetical.

2023

COMMANDER AND THIEF

Who, are we to believe, all we hear are lies.
Integrity is thrown out the door, we realize.
Nothing is sacred and meant to be the truth.
It's only a game so we're the pawns of ruse.

Who, are we to trust, when they, don't care.
They think we are ignorant, that is their lair.
But the joke is now a commander and chief.
For the truth is, he's a commander and thief.

2024

CITIZENS REIGN

We are the ones, who are, in charge of this land.
Not politicians who believe they make demands.
On American citizens when they are ones below.
And should respect our wishes in what we know.
The truth of the matter is they take power to gain.
But seem to forget who's in charge citizens reign.

2024

LIES THE TRUTH

There is truth within a lie
For it reveals a soul's eye

To see who they truly are
One need not go very far

As the lies begin to grow
The person begins to show

Integrity never comes out
When those lies are about

2012

PROSPERITY AND POWER

Money is the source for a political career to grow.
For, it is the root of the problem that doesn't show.
Who knows, where the paper trail, will come from.
They're living the high life not caring our outcome.
When, we elected them, be our voice, a democracy.
They become rich was not the plan, their prosperity.

Control the objective, for a political career to grow.
For, it is the root of the problem, that doesn't show.
Who knows where the mindset to rule, comes from.
They're living by rules for thee not for me outcome.
When, we elected them, abide one voice that's ours.
They become dictators was not the plan their power.

2024

DEATH OF DIALECTICS

Debate is dying there is no discussions anymore.
The matter is closed when no one wishes to explore.
A different opinion, than the one you hold on to.
And believing all others are mistaken without a clue.
It's a sad world when, freedom of thought, dies.
Maybe it's time to open our minds listen give it a try.

2024

NON-DISCLOSURE

There's no longer debate,
There is only hate!

2024

ELITE DEFEAT

Time has a way to eventually uncover their plans.

When, they think they have hidden their demands.

On society who they believe is sheep to be herded.

But little do they realize, we are aware and alerted.

To their, one world order, individuals are in defeat.

Let it be known we'll not be controlled by the elite.

2023

DECEPTION

Mark my word

Secrets, unheard

Do not stay hidden

Even the forbidden

Lies of deception

A life's reflection

In time, one purpose

Comes to the surface

2006

SOVEREIGNTY

There is a difference, when ruling our nation.
We have no monarch to dictate at this station.
By a supreme ruler who thinks they're a boss.
Of us all, without thought, what it might, cost.

Get off your high horse, start walking the line.
As a politician, means get behind us, this time.
We are the ones to rule, our nation, we believe.
There is no room for sovereignty if we are free.

2024

CHOOSE

Which, door do you choose for our country to take.

The door you choose will be for our country's sake.

Do, you turn the knob, to keep democracy the prize.

Or will you open the door and hypocrisy is realized.

We better be careful if we choose a new way of life.

For, once the door is opened liberty dies by its knife.

2024

MADNESS OF THE MASSES

When more than two or three gather there it can be.
It's beginning something stirring within a gathering.
Emotions are flying like the irrational flames in fire.
Once it is ignited there's little one can do by its dire.

2024

MANIC

It doesn't surprise me that man is in manic.
When, we are the cause of chaos and panic.
It's our wild and deranged excitement from.
Thinking our insane ideas are the only ones.
Let's get off its high horse and be grounded.
And come to our senses so sanity's founded.

2024

ABSOLUTE

Some may say there are no absolutes.
And rule of law should be what suits.
But that's not living with a sane mind.
It seems like insanity has taken shrine.

And rule of chaos is becoming a norm.
Society must wake up and be informed.
For absolutely there should be the law.
It keeps us from being as an animal all.

2024

WAKE UP

I'm afraid we have fallen asleep
And apathetic to those who weep

As they fight for what is so right
To be able to battle, one's blight

When, our liberty is taken away
Will, we be on our guard, today

And not be asleep as the corrupt
Take over our freedom, wake up

2023

AWAKEN

I woke up to find reality isn't real.

Life's not based on facts but how one feels.

Our eyes are wide shut being blind.

Thinking we see things clearly in our minds.

We are fooling ourselves and taken.

By a world that's not real we must be awaken.

2024

UPSIDE DOWN WORLD

Your beliefs are now the truth,

And mine are just a ruse.

Your feelings we all must share,

But mine you do not care.

Your actions are not for good,

And mine's misunderstood.

Your world is upside down,

But mine it's no longer around.

2023

OXYMORON

YOU WILL OWN NOTHING
YOU WILL OWE EVERYTHING

2024

BE VIGILANT

One must protect the sanctity of their freedom.
If not careful liberty may have wrong outcome.
For our country that was founded with all to be.
In a land of opportunity if its citizens to be free.
So be on guard and keep a watchful eye to those.
Who wish to take away liberty, they're exposed.

2024

BE DILIGENT

One must never give up fighting for freedom.
If not careful, it may be, taken from someone.
For, our country is founded, so all can be free.
In this land of opportunity, all citizens will be.
So be on guard to protect it, by being vigilant.
Who wish to take away our liberty be diligent.

2024

NO LONGER BE

We will, no longer be lied to.
We will, no longer be told who.
We will, no longer be like sheep.
We will, no longer be in defeat.
We will, no longer be in denial.
We will, no longer be on trial.
We will, no longer be kept down.
We will, no longer be not around.
We will, no longer be forlorn.
We will, no longer be uninformed.
We will, no longer be your slave.
We will, no longer be not brave.

2024

COLLATERAL CATTLE

Humanity is on the chopping block today.
And just like trees we are lumber as prey.
One by one gathered like sheep in a yard.
As freedom is sold we better be on guard.
For, the wolves are in charge of the cattle.
We are nothing but collateral in this battle.

2022

AMONG US

Who, can be against us, when they are among us.
Together we are a nation of differences, and trust.
We will come together to the good of our country.
This is our only chance to live a freedom's liberty.

No one is better, those among us, for we are same.
When we all want the same outcome a life's game.
To live the best we can, and to share, that we must.
And not to be afraid to say what we feel among us.

2024

SILENTLY SPEAKING

They are not in numbers, standing, behind picket lines.
They, stay behind taking care those, not meant, to find.
They work hard for family, and don't speak their mind.
They're silently speaking the American dream to climb.

2024

FREEDOM BE

LET THE BELLS OF FREEDOM BE
RINGING IN OUR COUNTRY FOR YOU AND ME

2024

CRIES OF DECEPTION

It's in the wind that I hear your cry.
For, there's no truth only one's lies.
As they blow in the breeze they fly.
Away from me now that I'll realize.
For, there's no truth only one's lies.
It's in the wind that I hear your cry.

2023

ABBA vs. ALLAH
(Alien vs. Predator)

Within a world's stage two forces soon will meet.
They come upon the stage their forces set to beat.

To destroy and conquer this winner will take all.
Their mission is to conquer us the sinner in us all.

For, one we will bow to which name do we call.
Bow in prayer for Jehovah or on knees for Allah.

They come upon the stage their forces set to beat.
Within a world's stage two forces soon will meet.

2009

REMEMBER SEPTEMBER

There were blue skies

And rain cloud cries

There were trees blowing

And end of summer showing

There were many faces

And hometown places

There were smiles to see

And sadness will be

There were planes in the sky

And love ones to die

That day in September

We must always remember

2012

RECIPE FOR DISASTER

      1 lb. HATE   1 large Policy
      1 lb. LIES   1 to 4 Politicians
   Ground Together   1 tsp Corruption
   6 Cups of Media   and a pinch of
   2 ½ Cups Deceit   Apathy

1. Put media, corruption and apathy into a cooker and cook on high for an hour.
2. Stir in deceit, cover and cook on high for ½ hour.
3. Add hate and lies, 1 large policy and 1 to 4 politicians mix well. Cover and cook on low for another hour.
4. Uncover if not distributed enough cook a little longer stirring up emotions.
5. When done place in every home and feed the masses.

2024

WARFARE'S MENU

APPETIZERS

Potato Skins - an epidermis nightshade constituting suppression
Cheese Styx - a temptress seduction of man with devilish suavity
Shrimp Cocktail - a sardonic person cloned to construct terrorism
Crab Dip - a political concoction of mismatched dire convictions

ALA CARTE
Each Entree Includes Islamic Extremist Victims

Middle Eastern Cuisine - hometown favorite hotplate of flames
16 oz. T. Bone Steak - country grazed 100% All American Beef
English Pot Pie - a hearty stew that will stay true to one's allies
Spaghetti and Meatballs - a steadfast Italian inflexible with balls
Oriental Stir Fry - a mixture of flavors from the Orient for peace
Chicken Cordon Bleu - an international venue takes French leave
Bratwurst / Sauerkraut - a bitter Kraut with tail between his legs
Stroganoff - a Russian delicacy known not to keep with sanctions
Spanish Rice Plate - crumbling of opinions via explosions too hot

DESSERTS

Apple Pie a la Mode - Everyone deserves their piece of the pie
Angel and Devil Cake - You can have your cake and eat it too

25 % gratuity is placed upon taxpayers

2004

FOOTSTEPS

I signed up for this, to fight for our bliss.
And while I'm gone I know I'll be missed.
I'm away from home, but, I am not alone.
My mission is clear and my life's on loan.
I put aside my fears, what I'm doing here.
When, I walk the footsteps of volunteers.

I know I may be going home, like a stone.
With a flag on a wooden box, I am not alone.
So shed no solemn tears, put aside your fears.
As I, walk the footsteps of fallen volunteers.
Who, kept our country strong from all wrong.
I signed up for this, and it is where I belong.

2007

FORTITUDE

Like a fort, that protects those within.
Be soldiers that negate their safety in.

This courage is armor they have worn.
And are the heroes who fight in a war.

2024

INDEBTEDNESS

In the middle of the night he kisses her cheek.
It is goodnight and goodbye for this he seeks.
He wanders to his son's bedroom in the dark.
This night will be his last to leave one's mark.
For tonight he is deployed with others to war.
He is a soldier for his country, a man of honor.

2004

A SOLDIER'S GLORY
(To Our Military)

He walks the line on a deserted street
And keeps a watchful eye whom he meets
He carries a weapon across his shoulder
His steady hand ready until his tour is over
But he walks the line not to cause harm
For, he walks the line to protect and to alarm
From those who will be our destruction
Their mission is to kill and stop construction
When, we build new roads and schools
For their country's future is by freedom's tools
So he walks the line with a watchful eye
The weapon he carries is so democracy can fly
And this soldier is there with a new story
As he walks the line it is for a soldier's glory

2008

TO MY SON
(A prayer to a Marine)

There is so much I want to say to you
When we pass by or I enter your room
Only our eyes can speak for each other
Unspoken words, meant for each other
Kept away, swept away, by one's tears
But, now, my son, I cry from my fears
I tried to be strong by showing strength
Because I know you will need strength
And I tried to be strong by giving praise
Because I know you'll be needing praise
And I've tried to be strong by not crying
But, now, my son, your chance of dying
Could, only be, kept away, swept away
By my prayer for you from all my fears
My unspoken words, free from all tears
So when we pass by or I enter your room
The words, I will say to you, I love you

2005

THANK YOU LETTER

November 11, 2005

To Our Military,

I am writing this letter, to thank you for your courage.
And hope to lighten the load, with words to encourage.
To all men and women in our armed forces harms way.
It's their daily unselfish sacrifices for our liberty today.
I pray for your safety may your skills keep your strong.
The war's soon over you'll be home where you belong.
But until then please remember my words of thank you.
Because of your valor we do fly the red, white and blue.

Thank you for our freedom,

An American Citizen

STAND UP

Stand up and be proud for this country of ours.

And salute the flag for the brave living under flowers.

For, they have died to insure our freedom here.

It's an insurance policy signed in blood fighting there.

So show deep respect to those wearing uniform.

By telling them "Thank you" is a small price to inform.

2024

TRIBUTE

Harms way

Their day

Make way

Every day

Find a way

Say today

Thank you

2005

IN REMEMBRANCE

In a news flash are the portraits, in memory of their faces.

Our nation's fallen force, from homeland's diverse places.

We must never forget the cost by remembering every name.

Their demise is a solemn moment in time with heroic fame.

2004

PRICE OF FREEDOM

Freedom is not free there is a price.
Of those that have fought with their life.
Many have died a sacrifice in blood.
As they follow from the example above.

We're so blessed to have heroes here.
By the brave souls who put away their fear.
And fight to make sure we are all free.
They to be remembered a freedom's decree.

2023

THE HOMECOMING

The day was almost here to when he'll be home.
A year's end was near, his wife won't be alone.
And three little girls will finally have their dad.
Together they're a family sad will now be glad.

Friends and relatives gather to celebrate a day.
When all who's there's happy he is on his way.
For that is what it's thought hoping to surprise.
But instead of him arriving, a knock is realized.

Two young men in uniform she sees at her door.
Not a loving husband, she'll never see, no more.
The day was almost near his homecoming stone.
A year's end was here a casket was now his home.

2023

CHRISTMAS LIST

1. World Peace
2. Hatred Wrong
3. Disease Deceased
4. Hunger Gone
5. Earth Spared
6. Unity Arise
7. Everyone Cares
8. Politics Dies

2005

FORGIVENESS

There is one undeniable truth to heal wounds afflicted.
Bare the venom of sin our fathers' inherited addicted.
Open the hearts of many by extending hands of mercy.
Hoping an out stretched hand seeks others mirthfully.
To look beyond our differences to see we are the same.
You and I the world's problem and we are all to blame.
Be the solution, the destruction of hatred in willingness.
We are amid angels to look upon man with forgiveness.

2004

REMEMBER THEM

Remember them, remember when
This nation began by minutemen
And a flag is torn but flew to stay
Still flying high on Memorial Day

Remember them, remember when
Our nation's brothers battled to win
In a Civil War, between the States
Be a reminder, this Memorial Day

Remember them, remember when
Our nation's sons by ocean's send
Fought World War I across the way
Be a reminder, this Memorial Day

Remember them, remember when
Our nation's courage is needed again
Fought World War II across the way
Be a reminder, this Memorial Day

Remember them, remember when
Our nation's freedom, a symbol in
The Korean War, the North strays
Be a reminder, this Memorial Day

2

Remember them, remember when
Our nation's draft takes men to fend
The war in Vietnam our men will lay
Be a reminder, this Memorial Day

Remember them, remember when
Our nation's sons and daughter then
Obeyed the call in the Gulf War days
Be a reminder, this Memorial Day

Remember them, remember when
Our nation's citizens band to mend
Terrorism tries to demise the USA
Be a reminder, this Memorial Day

Remember them, remember when
Our nation's strength is there to win
The War in Iraq, democracy's way
Be a reminder, this Memorial Day

Remember them, remember when
This nation began by minutemen
And a flag is torn but flew to stay
Still flying high on Memorial Day

2007

WE WILL STILL STRIVE

Don't take for granted the perseverance we possess
"Give me liberty or give me death," a forefather confessed
Many a men and women have fought to keep us free
And many more are more than willing today forever to be
One of the brave to fight for our freedom and even die
For this is the United States of America, we will still strive

2024

THE ULTIMATE SACRIFICE

They take a call in the middle of the night
For, they are sent to make a wrong right
With sirens screaming through the streets
Unaware by whom they will meet
And with each call their lives are in plight
Being officers of the law is the ultimate sacrifice

They take a call in the middle of the night
For, they are sent to drown a fire's light
With sirens raging through the streets
Unaware the blazing flames of heat
And with each call their lives are in fright
Being firefighters is their call the ultimate sacrifice

2

They take a call in the middle of the night
For, they are sent to know or die one might
With sirens crying through the streets
Unaware are the patients so weak
And with each call their lives are in flight
Being responders is their call the ultimate sacrifice

They take a call in the middle of the night
For, they are sent to a war zone to fight
With sirens roaring through the streets
Unaware whom the enemy might be
And with each call their lives are in blight
Being soldiers for us all is the ultimate sacrifice

2008

BEYOND DUTY

To the brave men and women who served this country.
We are indebted to you for the freedoms that we share.
Because of your bravery Lady Liberty won't be hungry.
For, simple things in life, her citizens, no doubt do care.
We are one nation and together we must stand with her.
And not to be divided, by issues, meant to tear us apart.
Don't be fooled by its wolves in sheep clothing that stir.
Up our emotions who try to keep us a stone in the heart.
It is our duty to go beyond and be like the brave we see.
They've sacrificed for our country by their death prayer.
There's no other place on Earth that's better I do believe.
So stand with her, not against her, united we will declare.

2023

EVENTUALLY

All is Fell

All is Hell

All is Jell

All is Well

2005

BEACON ON THE HILL

America's a light, in a dark of night.
She shines as stars to be seen from afar.
And she stands, steadfast, with honor fast.
With her courage she defends, and will lend.
To those lesser still, she's a beacon, on the hill.

2024

SO PROUD

I am so proud, of those that have served.
I am so proud, of a respect, they deserve.

I am so proud of my country we do share.
I am so proud of its flag, waves in the air.

I am so proud of the beauty surrounds me.
I am so proud of a freedom live and let be.

2024

ON THE HORIZON

A beacon on the hill shines for freedom's right.
For many fought to give their lives for the fight.
So you and I privileged to live in a country free.
We must never forget those who made this to be.
And as our flag a symbol for what has been won.
This nation gives hope tomorrow on the horizon.

2024

NOTEWORTHY

Take notice of this great country of ours.
Of its beauty of its landscapes that showers.
Like the dew on a flower ready to bloom.
We have so much to be thankful for, whom.

Take notice of this great country we share.
Of its generosity to others and don't compare.
Like the people who give, to help, in need.
We have so much, to be thankful for, indeed.

2023

SO THANKFUL

I am so thankful for the many blessings here.
I am so thankful for a freedom that we share.
I am so thankful for glorious mountains high.
I am so thankful for the magnificent blue sky.
I am so thankful for sandy beaches by the sea.
I am so thankful for oceans, lakes, rivers, free.
I am so thankful for the trees in forests nearby.
I am so thankful for the beautiful birds that fly.
I am so thankful for the bountiful animals out.
I am so thankful for the walks and talks about.
I am so thankful for its many people who care.
I am so thankful for America a home we share.

2024

HOME COOKING

There's nothing better than a home cooked meal.
When it comes from the heart, and simmers still.
Until, it is done and ready for family to consume.
They sit around the table saying prayers assumed.

We should be thankful for all the blessings today.
From farmers to the ranchers, and those who stay.
To make sure we are bountiful, with plenty to eat.
America will welcome ones grateful for their seat.

2024

LAND OF THE GIVING

How generous are we, to keep giving, and giving.
When other countries I see, care less for the living.
They'd rather build up their military might instead.
Not to feed the hungry but make room for the dead.

America has her faults no country is without blame.
But at least we are compassionate to help is the aim.
And share our good fortune, to those, that are living.
We take care of our brother in the land of the giving.

2024

STAND TALL

I am proud, of this country, the United States.
Even with past discretions being up to debate.
No nation is perfect but we'll strive to the call.
To help those in need. I'll stand proud and tall.

2024

THE CHOSEN

One who thinks it is coincidental we are the United States.
Should think again for there's a reason that we are so great.
We have been chosen from above with God's blessing here.
So we must share our good fortune, with those without fear.

To become part of the family we welcome them to the table.
But in order to dine with us they must prove they to be able.
And share our good fortune, by not trying to destroy liberty.
For that is why we have been chosen as the home of the free.

2024

MONUMENTAL

One need not look very far, when looking, at this country of ours.
As the Lord has blessed her with abundance of gifts He showered.

The vast landscapes are painted with God's beautiful tones of color.
And forests of green will be decorated in autumn hues like no other.

Majestic mountains blcom like a flower though they reach the stars.
As they invite the explorer to climb their height, hoping they go far.

And lakes, rivers, oceans of fish, sparkle like the dazzling diamond.
We're enriched with our country's beauty one must take the time in.

2024

HOME BLESSED

No other place in the world I'd rather be.
But just right here where I know I'm free.
Yes it's nice to travel and see other sights.
It is good to be home, where I have rights.
With beauty beyond, I will make my nest.
My home is America, I am, home blessed.

2024

GRATITUDE

Look around and see the spacious skies.
Look around and see a beauty here arise.

Look around and see its forests of green.
Look around and see this freedom brings.

Look around and see majestic mountains.
Look around and see lifted spirits abound.

Look around and see the many faces near.
Look around and see gratitude, to be here.

2023

FREE AS A FISH

I am free as a fish swimming in the sea.

For that is how I wish, my liberty, to be.

So no fishing line will I swallow its lure.

To be caught in its net captured, for sure.

And be eaten by those who try to control.

How I live my life free it's how I snorkel.

2024

BEAUTIFUL, BEAUTIFUL

Beautiful are your vast landscapes.
Beautiful are your rivers and lakes.
Beautiful are your mountains high.
Beautiful are your blue green skies.
Beautiful are your fields with grain.
Beautiful are your storms from rain.
Beautiful are your flowers in bloom.
Beautiful are your nights by a moon.
Beautiful are your animals in a wild.
Beautiful are your dreams of a child.
Beautiful are your citizens of liberty.
Beautiful are your rights we are free.

2024

SKY HIGH

It is surrounded by beauty of majestic skies.
Its hues bound by a duty, magnificent dyes.

Pillars in length, reach out toward the stars.
Willows in strength, teach forward inwards.

A sentry to the level land, sheltered to wind.
Centuries as a bevel stand, filtered from sin.

Within this mountain, nature's creation cries.
Within this fountain, a love for elevation lies.

2004

CLIMB TO THE TOP

It is up to you how far you will climb.
The power is within if you take the time.
And give it your all for a future bright.
If you do what it takes a goal is in sight.
Don't look behind, for you, may stop.
You must look ahead, to climb to the top.

2024

MAKE MY WAY

It is up to me, how I should live.
How much I put in is what gives.
I can climb to success, at the top.
Or take it easy and progress stops.

I am the ruler of my own destiny.
There's no one to blame in equity.
Life's destination is how you play.
Happiness within, I make my way.

2024

BRAVE

This country began by those who fought.
For freedom they choose is what they sought.
Not to be ruled by a ruler taking all rights.
From the citizens that live, under their might.
We are the ones that govern this bold land.
When, we were the ones that made the stand.
And choose to be free by not being a slave.
We are America we're the home of the brave.

2024

THE BEST THERE IS

America is not perfect, but what other country is.
Look at history did they fight to end their slavery.
When thousands of our men died was the analysis.
They lay on the battlefield, is nothing but bravery.

America is not perfect but I wouldn't want to live.
Any where else in the world is better that I do see.
It's a country with all its faults still willing to give.
To those that are hoping, for their home to be free.

2024

AMERICA

Her land is so beautiful, from land to the sea
I need, only to open my eyes, then to believe
God has blessed her with abundance so great
With spacious blue skies and rivers and lakes
And majestic mountains, climb up to a height
That tells a glorious story of justice and might
In America, there is no other place I would be
When, she's so beautiful, and home of the free

2024

FREEDOM WITHIN

No one can take away my freedom within.
For, it is, apart, of my soul within my skin.
Every fiber of my being is stitched, with it.
The ones who have died I will never forget.

It is because of their bravery, we to be free.
As it is my life I live no one else can be me.
So no one can take my freedom it is within.
For, it's essence of my soul, within my skin.

2024

ROUNDABOUT

History seems to be a revolving door.
What's happening today happened before.

2024

LIFE, LIBERTY LESSONS

1. A human is a human no matter how small.
2. Get back, on the horse, if you, should fall.
3. No one's greater than the other, in the line.
4. Taking from others without asking a crime.
5. Trying to silence speech we cannot permit.
6. Destroying property, in protest is not legit.
7. Burning the flag disrespects ones who died.
8. Standing at attention for the pledge applied.
9. Show respect to men and women who serve.
10. Be proud of this country freedom's observe.

2024

SALUTE

A gesture of deep respect is not much to ask.
To those who've served our country, by task.
And wear their uniform to protect this nation.
From adversaries who try to destroy creation.

Of our freedom, we have in the United States.
So we must acknowledge the sacrifice it takes.
They go into battle to fight for liberty absolute.
We should pay homage, to our flag, and salute.

2024

ALLEGIANCE

Our nation, under God, I pledge allegiance to thee.
And to the flag that symbolizes that I'm to be free.
I am, proud of my country, for what she stands for.
And for the men and women who have died before.
To protect this land from those who despise liberty.
One must never forget, a price paid for you and me.

2024

ICONIC IMAGES

Thru out history there have been pictures that have last

It's test of time, to the present moment, from our past

In words The Star Spangled Banner our flag held high

By the brave patriots who kept her flying, as they died

To the Marines on Iowa Jima fought for freedom there

For, six young men, in honor raised our flag, with care

So sad there're those who try to tear down our Republic

And attempt to assassinate our nation's (45th) president

But once again, a picture, will be thru out history's time

His fist rising above his bloody face and our flag behind

2024

AMERICA STATE OF MIND

There are those who like to fly away on a holiday
Just to get away on a non stop flight to an Italian beach
Or to Istanbul, but me I'm taking a road trip on the
California coastline, I'm in an America state of mind

I've seen all the same ole stars not very far
From their antiquity scenes I've seen the Alps no lie
Just like our mountains high under the deep blue sky
But I know where I'm headed and I don't need
Much time, I'm in an America state of mind

I have it so easy living my way every day
Don't need too much to stay in touch
With no reasons to move but now I wish to
Take a break from life's hectic dues

I'm down with this and it's time
I've found some way to unwind
I don't care if it's a small town or
Along a river side there are no reasons to leave
Here when I find, I'm in an America state of mind

I'm just taking a road trip on the California coastline
Cause I'm in an America state of mind

2024

www.ingramcontent.com/pod-product-compliance
Lightning Source LLC
LaVergne TN
LVHW041707070526
838199LV00045B/1245